Miniature communication robot *Robi* can walk and even dance, as well as talk to humans.

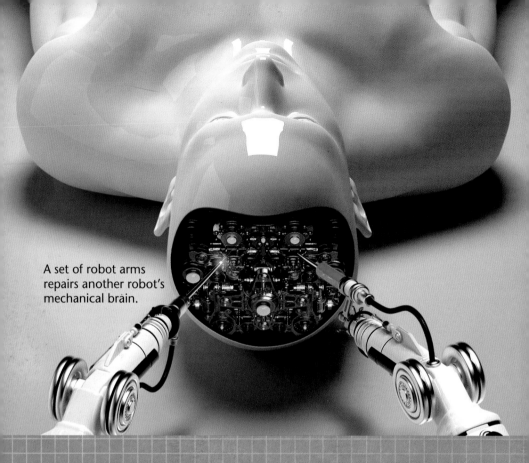

A set of robot arms repairs another robot's mechanical brain.

What is Artificial Intelligence?

The term *Artificial Intelligence*, or *A.I.* for short, was coined in the 1950s. It describes the idea of a machine that can show some form of intelligence – and, ideally, a machine that can think, learn and behave like a human being.

Although A.I. technology has come a long way, no one has achieved this ultimate goal – yet.

Today, computer coders can create simple versions of A.I. using step by step instructions known as *algorithms*. Different algorithms allow computers to carry out tasks that require a level of intelligence, such as playing games, translating text from one language to another, and even holding a conversation.

Getting connected

Some A.I. engineers are attempting to create artificial brains. Instead of designing algorithms, they create digital versions of the nerve cells, or *neurons*, that make up a human brain. If they succeed, artificial brains may one day even be able to think and feel as we do.

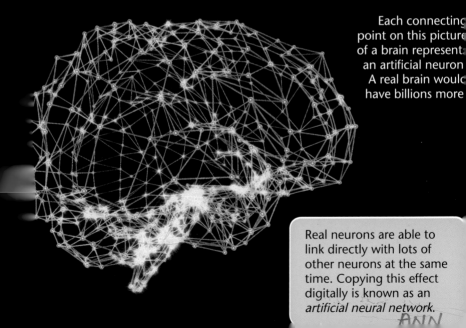

Each connecting point on this picture of a brain represents an artificial neuron. A real brain would have billions more.

Real neurons are able to link directly with lots of other neurons at the same time. Copying this effect digitally is known as an *artificial neural network*.

ANN

Strong and weak

Most machines, including robots, are designed to perform a *single* task. Even if it is a fairly complicated one, it's classified as *narrow* or *weak A.I.* Machines that can do *many* jobs and at the same level of skill as a human are described as having *general* or *strong A.I.*

Many experts claim that strong A.I. hasn't been invented yet. But even weak A.I. can sometimes be enough to give machines abilities well beyond a human, or even a team of humans.

Weak A.I. in action

These robots are using A.I. to sort objects by shape as they move along a conveyor belt. They can do this job faster and more accurately than any human.

But if you ask the robots to sort the objects by their weight, thickness or some other quality, they don't know how.

Strong A.I. is likely to require immense computing power, probably using a machine called a *supercomputer*. Supercomputers combine the power of several million 'normal' desktop computers.

China's top supercomputer, *Tianhe II*, is the most powerful computing machine in the world. It's made up of cabinets filled with microchips and circuitry that fill an area roughly the size of a tennis court.

orking alone

The most basic forms of A.I. give robots the
power to solve simple problems by themselves.

This ground robot is searching a damaged building.
The first command is simply to move forward.

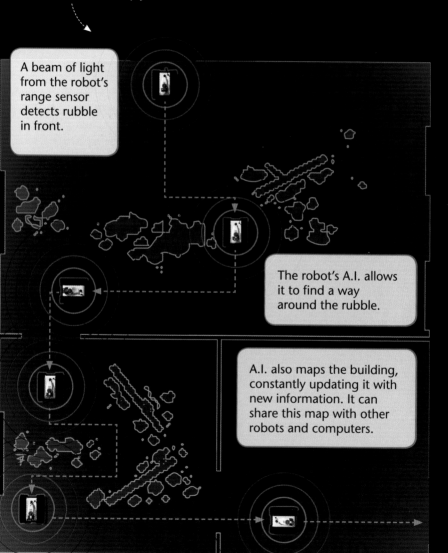

A beam of light
from the robot's
range sensor
detects rubble
in front.

The robot's A.I. allows
it to find a way
around the rubble.

A.I. also maps the building,
constantly updating it with
new information. It can
share this map with other
robots and computers.

This kind of basic A.I. only allows the robot to solve problems that it has been programmed to expect. It might struggle with an *unexpected* situation, such as animals that occasionally move around and block its path.

This robot, a Moon rover named *Lunokhod 1*, is still in development.

Engineers are designing A.I. software that will allow it to make decisions about which way to move to avoid obstacles, and what samples to collect.

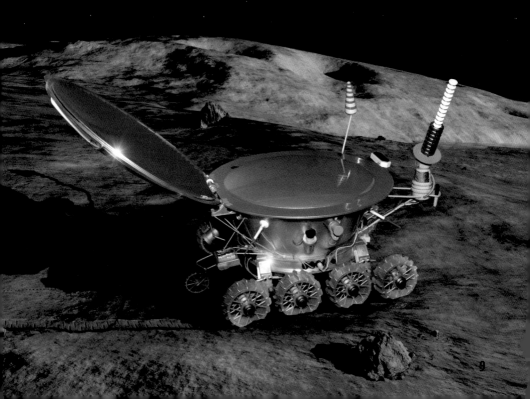

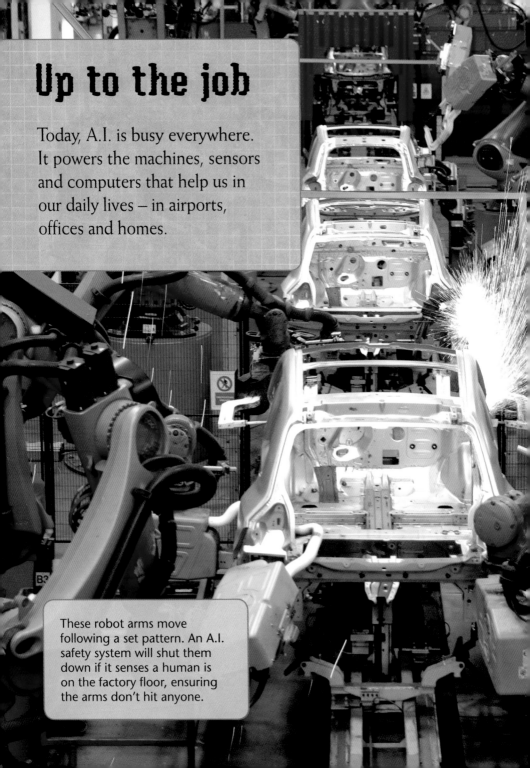

Up to the job

Today, A.I. is busy everywhere. It powers the machines, sensors and computers that help us in our daily lives – in airports, offices and homes.

These robot arms move following a set pattern. An A.I. safety system will shut them down if it senses a human is on the factory floor, ensuring the arms don't hit anyone.

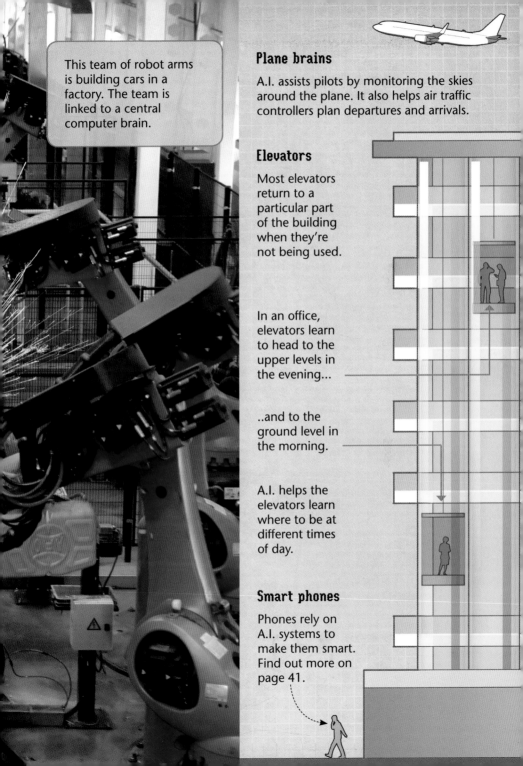

This team of robot arms is building cars in a factory. The team is linked to a central computer brain.

Plane brains

A.I. assists pilots by monitoring the skies around the plane. It also helps air traffic controllers plan departures and arrivals.

Elevators

Most elevators return to a particular part of the building when they're not being used.

In an office, elevators learn to head to the upper levels in the evening...

..and to the ground level in the morning.

A.I. helps the elevators learn where to be at different times of day.

Smart phones

Phones rely on A.I. systems to make them smart. Find out more on page 41.

Stone tools to robots

One of the first signs that early humans were intelligent was that they made and used tools. Over the course of millions of years, people learned to refine tool-making in all sorts of sophisticated ways.

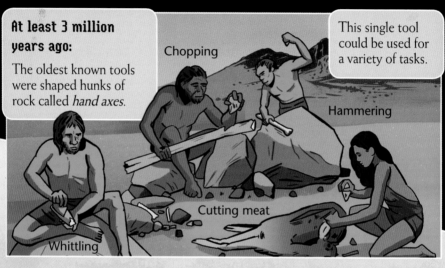

At least 3 million years ago:

The oldest known tools were shaped hunks of rock called *hand axes*.

Chopping

This single tool could be used for a variety of tasks.

Hammering

Cutting meat

Whittling

Around 250,000 years ago:

In time, people started to develop a variety of tools designed to carry out specific jobs.

Shell opener

Barbed speartip

Shaped oar

Around 20,000 years ago:

Many generations later, people built some of the oldest known *machines* – tools with moving parts.

Axle with wheels – for carrying heavy loads

Rope and pulley

Axle

Bow – for firing arrows

A little over 100 years ago:

Inventors combined multiple machines to make tools that could make themselves move.

This sketch shows a design for the first motor car, built by Karl Benz in the 1880s.

Fuel engine

Axle with wheels

20th century

A later innovation was to build machines that could be programmed (for a limited range of tasks), such as washing machines.

21st century

Many experts believe we are close to inventing robots that can complete all sorts of jobs by themselves.

I CAN TEA MYSELF!

Better than human?

No machine on Earth comes close to the power and incredible complexity of the human brain. The skills and senses most of us take for granted represent some of the greatest challenges for A.I. designers.

Computers versus humans	
What computers can do best	**What humans can do best (for now)**
• Carry out repetitive tasks, without making mistakes • Predict possible moves in games such as chess • Read and write at high speed • Remember vast amounts of information • Make incredibly fast calculations, without making mistakes • Follow orders exactly	• Notice when major mistakes have been made • Pick up and move pieces in any board game • Decipher human handwriting • Decide which information is worth remembering • Understand the purpose of performing a calculation • Use common sense to ignore orders that don't seem right

Understanding information

Our brains need bodies and senses to collect information about the outside world. Computer programs, or *software*, rely on machine parts and electronic components, known as *hardware*. In a computer, hardware and software combine to process information, usually called *data*.

Making sense of the world

Most robots are fitted with measuring tools called *sensors*. A.I. systems compare data that comes in through these sensors with stored data that explains what the sensors show. This allows the robot to make choices.

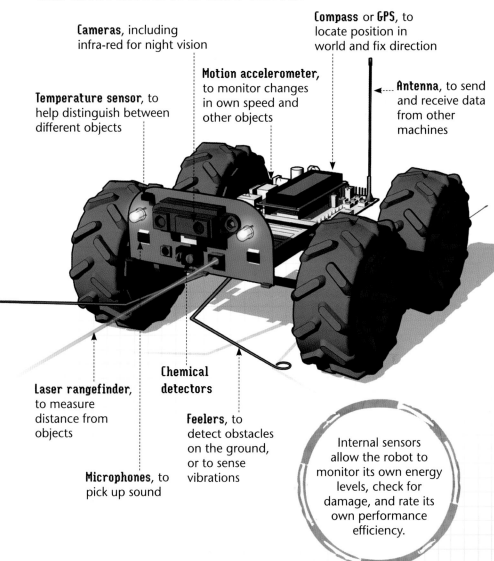

Cameras, including infra-red for night vision

Compass or **GPS,** to locate position in world and fix direction

Motion accelerometer, to monitor changes in own speed and other objects

Temperature sensor, to help distinguish between different objects

Antenna, to send and receive data from other machines

Laser rangefinder, to measure distance from objects

Chemical detectors

Feelers, to detect obstacles on the ground, or to sense vibrations

Microphones, to pick up sound

Internal sensors allow the robot to monitor its own energy levels, check for damage, and rate its own performance efficiency.

15

Imitating life

For thousands of years, craftsmen and inventors have been building machines that can move by themselves, known as *automata*. Many were originally designed to trick observers into thinking these machines were – in some sense – alive.

Singing birds (2,000 years ago)

Hero of Alexandria, in Egypt, was an inventor who used water and wind to power machines, such as this singing bird device.

1 Water falls from the spout into a pipe.

2 The water pushes air along the pipe...

3 ...and up through a whistle hidden in the bird's mouth, making it sing.

The Scribe (18th century)

Swiss clockmaker Pierre Jacquet-Droz built an automaton in the shape of a child sitting at a desk.

By marking up and feeding cards into a slot at the back, the machine could write sentences on paper, using pen and ink.

Elephant clock (10th century)

Arab scholar Al-Jazari designed over 100 mechanical contraptions, including many automata. Engineers today have built many of them, following Al-Jazari's detailed writings and drawings.

Hidden inside this elephant clock, a bowl of water fills up slowly. When the bowl is full, a set of strings makes the drummer signal the passing of each half-hour. Another string empties the bowl so it can fill up again.

Automata follow a fixed sequence of movements. Unlike robots with A.I., they cannot adapt or change that sequence to meet new situations.

Drummer

The first robot

The word *robot* comes from a play about mechanical people built as slaves, written by Czech author Karel Čapek in 1920.

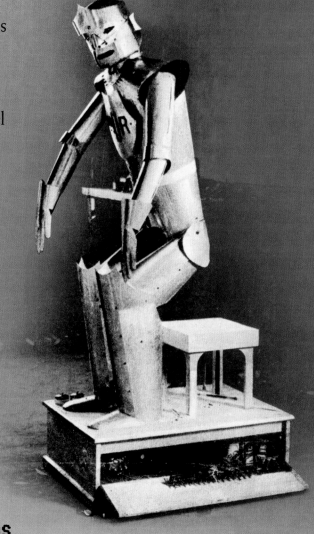

This robot was built for a 1929 production of Čapek's play *R.U.R.*

Any machine with arms, eyes or other features that resemble a person is described as a *humanoid robot*.

Artificial humans

Engineers today are working on robots that resemble people more and more closely. Science fiction stories often feature characters known as *androids* – robots so lifelike they're almost impossible to distinguish from humans.

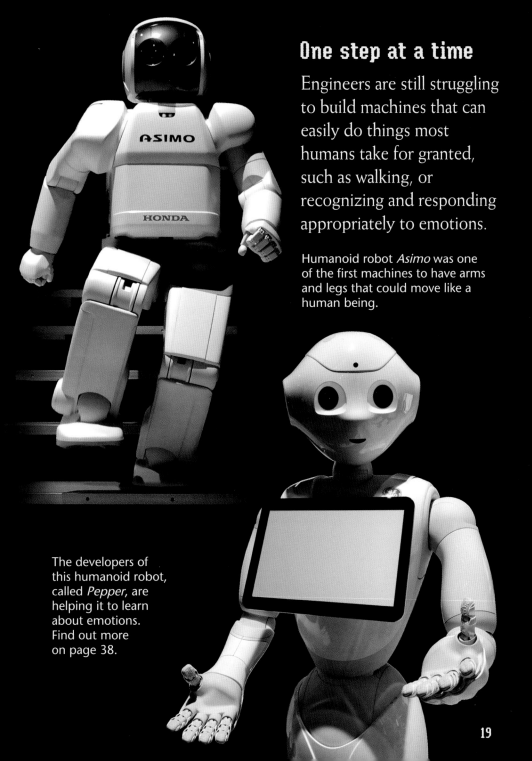

One step at a time

Engineers are still struggling to build machines that can easily do things most humans take for granted, such as walking, or recognizing and responding appropriately to emotions.

Humanoid robot *Asimo* was one of the first machines to have arms and legs that could move like a human being.

The developers of this humanoid robot, called *Pepper,* are helping it to learn about emotions. Find out more on page 38.

The birth of computers

Early inventors built automata to entertain and amaze. But, in the 1800s, British thinker and engineer Charles Babbage began work on a machine with a clear purpose: to solve almost any mathematical problem.

An error-free engine

In Babbage's day, people relied on tables of printed answers to complex calculations. But these tables often contained mistakes.

So he designed a machine, known as the *Difference Engine*, to perform and print reliable number tables.

Babbage began work on his engine in 1822, but never finished it. A working version, shown here, was built in the 1980s.

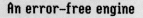

Each column of the machine was fitted with cogs, whose teeth were numbered from 0-9.

Users turned the handle the required number of times to perform a calculation.

Thinking bigger

Babbage abandoned his *Difference Engine* to design a new, more complicated machine: the *Analytical Engine*. Sadly, he never managed to build it.

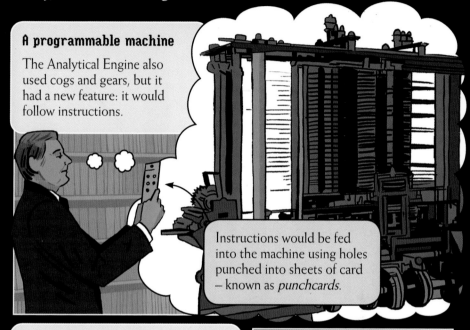

A programmable machine

The Analytical Engine also used cogs and gears, but it had a new feature: it would follow instructions.

Instructions would be fed into the machine using holes punched into sheets of card – known as *punchcards*.

These punchcards are the oldest known computer programs. Many were drawn up by Ada Lovelace, a mathematician and friend of Babbage's.

Could this machine be intelligent?

We'll never know!

The problem solvers

Almost a century after Babbage died, two mathematicians took up the challenge of creating the ultimate tool – a machine that could solve problems *beyond* mathematics.

Alan Turing (UK, 1912–1954)

Turing imagined a machine that could, potentially, answer *any* question.

The trick was to turn that question into a series of instructions. By working through the right algorithms, such a machine could solve the original problem all by itself.

John von Neumann (Hungary/USA, 1903–1957)

Von Neumann was among the first to understand how to assemble an actual machine – nowadays called a computer – that could work through complex algorithms.

To this day, the way components inside a computer are linked together is known as *Von Neumann architecture*.

War heroes

Both men had a crucial role in the Second World War (1939-1945). Von Neumann helped create the first atomic bombs, while Turing devoted many years to code-breaking.

Turing's *Bombe*

Turing helped design and build a computer-like machine known as the *Bombe*. It used a series of dials and switches to work methodically through messages written in a German wartime code named *Enigma*.

The Enigma code was updated on a daily basis, but the *Bombe* was always able to decipher the code – something a team of dedicated human code-breakers had failed to do.

The *Bombe* only worked to decipher Enigma-coded messages. But its success inspired colleagues to design machines that could be programmed to crack a variety of different codes.

The first true computers

In the late 1940s, work by Turing, Von Neumann and others led to the invention of electronic computers. These enormous machines could be programmed to solve different problems, often by following algorithms written onto punchcards.

Turing's intelligence test

Turing wasn't sure if a machine could ever match the power of a human brain, but he did believe that a machine could be called 'intelligent' if it was able to hold a human conversation.
He suggested a simple way to test that level of intelligence:

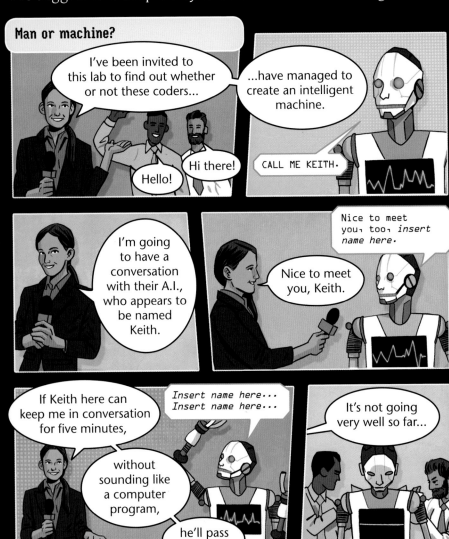

Failing the test

Some computer programs *have* successfully passed Turing's five-minute test. But, so far, no machine has been able to sustain a human-level conversation for more than a few minutes before it becomes obvious that it's not a person.

How to pass the test

Conversation algorithms use two main tricks.

1. The programmer inputs a list of typical questions and answers.

   This A.I. ought to work – at least, until a person makes a statement instead of asking a question.

2. The A.I. is linked to the internet. Whatever question a person asks, the A.I. will search for a similar question on a website and simply copy a typical answer.

   The more people talk to each other on the internet, the more likely the A.I. is to find a match.

Smaller and faster

Modern computers process billions of pieces of data every second. This incredible speed is a major part of what may push A.I. beyond human-level intelligence. The secret to this speed lies in tiny electronic components that make up the hardware.

1st generation computers
1940s–1950s

The first electronic computers were made of thousands of thumb-sized glass *valves*, and stored all their data on punchcards.

Valve, also called a *vacuum tube*, shown at actual size

2nd generation computers
1950s–1960s

Valves were replaced with much smaller components called *transistors*. Memory could be stored on thin strips of magnetic tape.

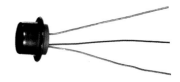

Transistor shown at actual size

3rd generation computers
1960s–1970s

Engineers combined multiple transistors into a single miniature circuit board. Technically known as *integrated circuits*, they are now more commonly called *microchips*.

Modern microchips can contain billions of microscopically small transistors, and are able to process and store vast amounts of data.

Prototype integrated circuit, patented by Jack Kilby of Texas Instruments in 1958, shown at actual size

4th generation computers
1979–present day

Combining sets of microchips onto a larger circuit called a *motherboard* led to the first computers small enough to fit onto a desk.

The *Commodore PET* 2001 was one of the first computers for sale, intended for home use.

How computers work

Valves and transistors act as switches, set to 'on' or 'off', or as 1 and 0.

By changing switches in a sequence, defined by an algorithm, computers can store and compare data.

Changing millions of switches at high speeds is what allows computers to solve problems almost instantaneously.

How fast?

Computer speed is measured in 'floating operations per second', or *flops* – roughly, how many lines of an algorithm different types of computers can work through in a second.

Machine	Era	Processing speed
Valve computer	1940s	500 flops
Transistor computer	1950s	Over 1 million flops
Early home computer	1980s	Over 100 million flops
Present-day laptop	2010s	Over 10 billion flops
Best supercomputer	2010s	Over 20 quadrillion flops

...of the game

...y beaten humans at one of our greatest thinking
game of chess. Some hail this as a victory for
...gence. Others have suggested instead that
...ess doesn't require true intelligence.

Machine victory

In 1997, supercomputer *Deep
Blue* defeated the world chess
champion Garry Kasparov.

The computer was able to
examine 200 million different
positions every second.

There are too many possible moves in a
chess game even for a supercomputer to
examine all of them. Instead, the A.I.
considers only the most promising moves.

Unbeatable machines

Since 2005, no solo player has beaten an A.I. in a chess tournament. Even grandmasters cannot help but make tiny mistakes, or choose to make a move that is not just about winning. They are human, after all.

Winning every time

Some A.I.s have discovered a series of steps that *guarantees* victory when playing games of skill such as draughts (or checkers), and even games of luck such as poker.

Type of game	Who's the best?
Othello / Reversi	A.I. since 1980s
Draughts / checkers	A.I. since 1980s
Scrabble™	A.I. since 1990s
Chess	A.I. since 1990s
Poker	A.I. since 2010s
Rock, Paper, Scissors	A.I. since 2012
Go	A.I. since 2016

A winning combination

Some grandmasters have chosen to harness the power of A.I. to make their own chess stronger.

In *freestyle* tournaments, players are encouraged to work in teams alongside the best chess programs.

Teams of humans and computers working together are sometimes known as *centaurs*. The name comes from creatures in Greek mythology that were half-human, half-horse.

Multi-gaming

The best human players can play simultaneous chess against hundreds of other players, rushing from board to board. But they can't match chess programs, which can play *millions* of simultaneous games.

Teaching learning

A.I. research teams, such as Google's DeepMind, are developing programs that can teach themselves to play all sorts of games, even ones they don't recognise. Early trials involved an old computer game known as *Atari® Breakout®*.

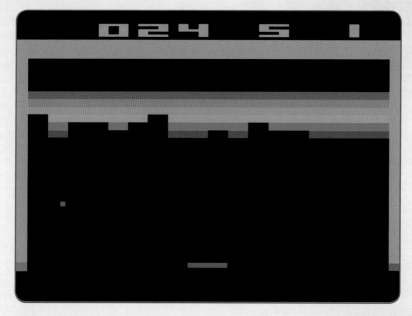

The aim of *Breakout®* is to smash all the bricks by bouncing a ball off a bat. If the bat misses the ball, the game is over.

Copycat champions

DeepMind's A.I. algorithms are not programmed to know the rules – their aim is simply to get the highest possible score. Different versions use different tactics. But those that copy players, human or A.I., have proved to be the fastest learners.

Mind games

Game designers are constantly pushing the limits of technology to develop games on phones, consoles and computers. A.I. can make imaginary worlds more lifelike, unpredictable and exciting.

Inside the game

Games played by people wearing headsets are sometimes described as *virtual reality*, or *VR*. The best use false sensory information beamed directly into the eyes and ears, giving the impression of being in another world.

This player is wearing a *PlayStation VR* headset.

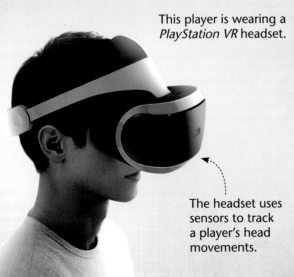

The headset uses sensors to track a player's head movements.

In this demo for a game called *The Deep*, players experience lifelike encounters with sea creatures such as manta rays.

A.I. engineering allows the game to adjust its virtual environment in direct response to the players' movements.

33

Teamwork

A.I. developers around the world compete in an annual event known as *RoboCup*, in which teams of humanoid robots play soccer. What would be a simple skill for humans requires a combination of complex engineering and A.I. coding.

NAO
(Aldebaran robotics,
2007–present)

- **height:** 58cm (23in)
- **running time:** 90 mins
- **top speed:** 0.3km/h (0.2mph)

All RoboCup games are played using *NAO* robots, of matching size and speed.

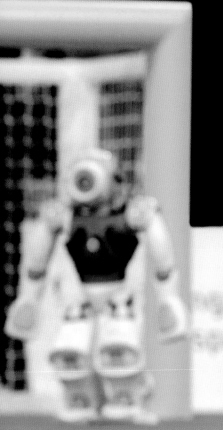

Human controllers input A.I. programs. But once the game is underway the robots operate entirely autonomously.

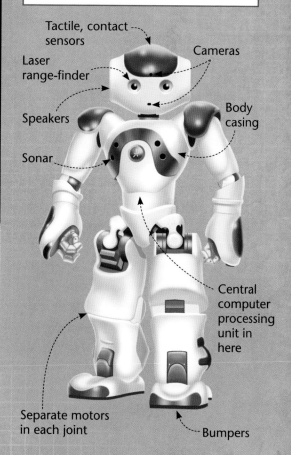

Tactile, contact sensors

Cameras

Laser range-finder

Speakers

Body casing

Sonar

Central computer processing unit in here

Separate motors in each joint

Bumpers

Until 2007, RoboCup tournaments were played by robot dogs known as *AIBO*.

Metal friends

Some toys, often known as *smart toys*, use A.I. to imitate pets, so that they will respond to human touch, movement or sound in a natural-seeming way. Some can even develop features of a personality, making them more lifelike still.

Robotic dogs, such as *Zoomer*™, use A.I. to to respond to voice commands. They can bark, roll over, follow their owners and perform other tricks, too.

The CogniToys *Dino* is a Wi-Fi connected, educational smart toy for children aged 5-9. Powered by IBM *Watson* and Elemental Path's *Friendgine* technology, the Dino can tell stories, play games and answer all sorts of questions.

Tamagotchi is a virtual pet. The creature on the screen is made using very simple A.I. that makes it cry when hungry or lonely. Owners have to use their own intelligence to care for the pet, pressing buttons to feed it and play with it.

Life-size companions

Humanoid robots can provide companionship as well as doing work. But some people find the most lifelike can be unsettling. This disturbing effect is known as *uncanny valley*, when something appears close to, but not quite, true to life.

This humanoid robot, named *Kobian,* is responding to sad news. With A.I., it has learned how to display seven distinct emotions.

Motors in the head allow *Kobian* to move its lips, eyes and neck in direct response to input from its sensors.

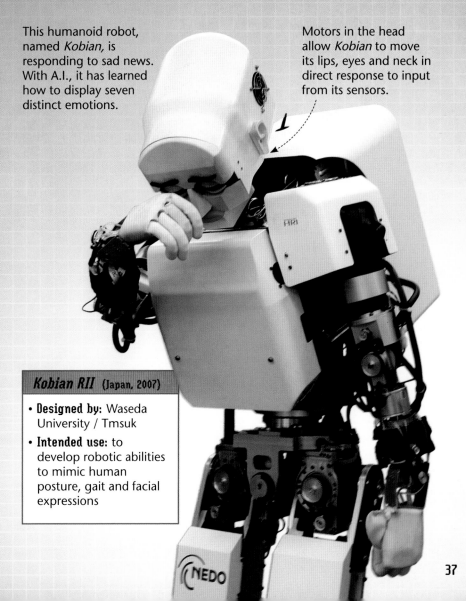

Kobian RII (Japan, 2007)

- **Designed by:** Waseda University / Tmsuk
- **Intended use:** to develop robotic abilities to mimic human posture, gait and facial expressions

Learning from humans

Robots with A.I. can improve their communication skills by watching and listening to people interacting with each other. This process also helps researchers understand the kind of jobs that humanoid robots might do in the future.

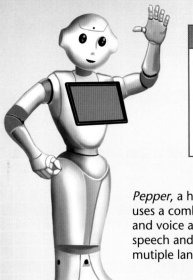

Pepper (France/Japan, 2014)

- **Designed by:** Aldebaran Robotics and SoftBank Mobile
- **Intended use:** interaction with people. In particular, it can recognize emotions and respond to them to help people feel better.

Pepper, a humanoid robot, uses a combination of cameras and voice analysis to react to speech and emotion – in mutiple languages.

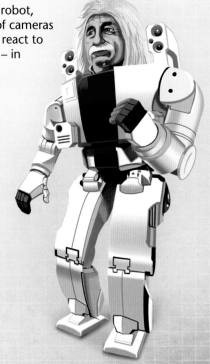

HUBO (South Korea, 2005)

- **Designed by:** Korea Advanced Institute of Science and Technology
- **Intended use:** mimicking human senses and movement

This HUBO android has been fitted with the face of Albert Einstein, designed by Dr. David Hanson. The face is flexible enough to make 30 expressions.

Getting a reaction

Humans instinctively respond to each other by reading and copying body language and facial expressions. Designers have given some robots human faces, to see if it makes people feel more comfortable talking to them.

Han (USA, 2010s)

- **Designed by:** Dr. David Hanson
- **Intended use:** Exploring human-machine interactions

Cameras in the eyes and chest allow *Han* to track and recognize faces.

40 separate motors allow *Han* to create a wide range of expressions.

Han's A.I. allows him to learn by experience and interacting with people. What *Han* has learned is already being used to design new and better models.

Synthetic skin known as Frubber™

Talking back

A.I. programs and machines are a long way from mastering human language, with all its subtle meanings, metaphors, jokes and hints. But they're getting better at it. Engineers are already using A.I. to help answer spoken questions and find solutions in smartphone assistants such as Apple's *Siri*.

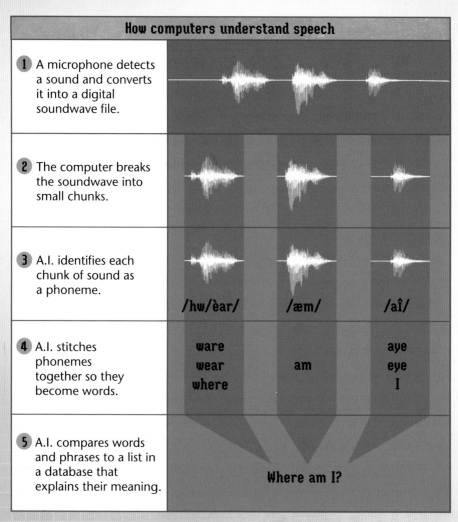

How computers understand speech			
1 A microphone detects a sound and converts it into a digital soundwave file.			
2 The computer breaks the soundwave into small chunks.			
3 A.I. identifies each chunk of sound as a phoneme.	/hw/èar/	/æm/	/aî/
4 A.I. stitches phonemes together so they become words.	ware wear where	am	aye eye I
5 A.I. compares words and phrases to a list in a database that explains their meaning.		Where am I?	

Most smartphones are able to answer simple spoken queries. The system is less like talking to a single intelligent person, and more like talking to a whole team of people.

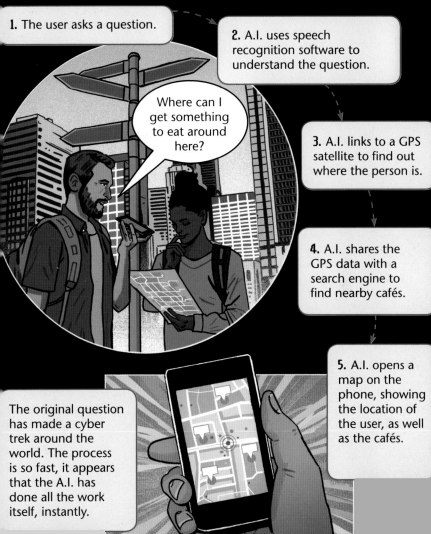

1. The user asks a question.

2. A.I. uses speech recognition software to understand the question.

Where can I get something to eat around here?

3. A.I. links to a GPS satellite to find out where the person is.

4. A.I. shares the GPS data with a search engine to find nearby cafés.

5. A.I. opens a map on the phone, showing the location of the user, as well as the cafés.

The original question has made a cyber trek around the world. The process is so fast, it appears that the A.I. has done all the work itself, instantly.

Robots in the workplace

In the future, machines with A.I. could assist
or replace humans working in all kinds of jobs.
Many creative people, from painters and
poets to musicians, are already using A.I. to
help them test and create new works of art.

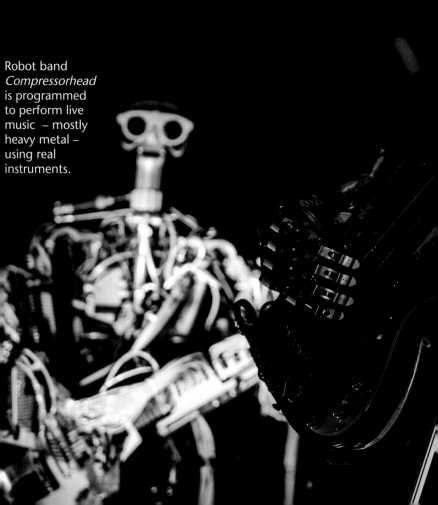

Robot band
Compressorhead
is programmed
to perform live
music – mostly
heavy metal –
using real
instruments.

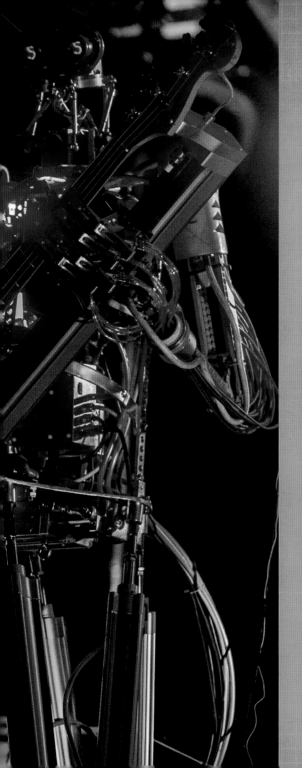

Is it art?

Robots fitted with cameras can be programmed to take photographs.

A new wave of A.I. software allows some robots to create paintings and drawings using traditional methods, too.

Painting by algorithm

Coder Harold Cohen has created A.I. software known as *AARON* that completes its own paintings.

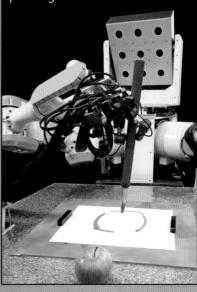

Flesh and blood

Surgeons are already using sophisticated machines to give them microscopically detailed control when performing operations. A new wave of A.I. systems can help doctors identify and even diagnose potential health problems.

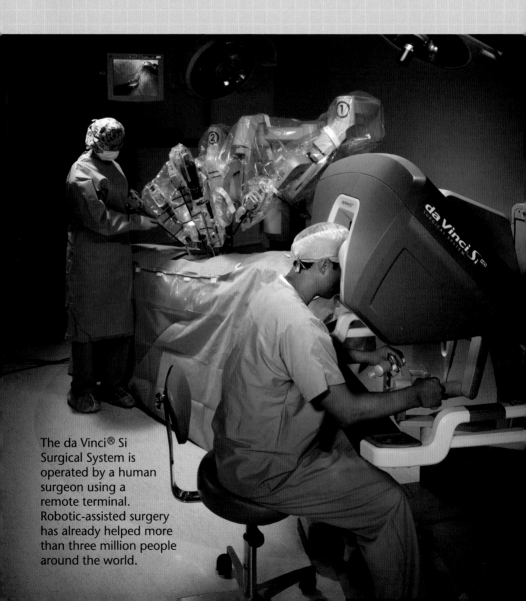

The da Vinci® Si Surgical System is operated by a human surgeon using a remote terminal. Robotic-assisted surgery has already helped more than three million people around the world.

Terapio (Japan, 2015)

- **Designed by:** Toyohashi University of Technology
- **Intended use:** medical assistance, recording basic patient data

Terapio is a mobile medical assistant, that can carry basic medical equipment as well as storing vital patient data.

Arms can pick up and carry a person.

ROBEAR (Japan, 2015)

- **Designed by:** RIKEN– Sumitomo Riko Collaboration
- **Intended use:** care for the elderly and basic nursing

ROBEAR's body is designed to navigate easily through a person's home.

IBM *Watson Health*™ (USA, 2006)

- **Developed by:** IBM
- **Intended use:** to support physicians as they care for patients by tapping into a database of medical information and listing evidence based treatment options.

Watson is the name of a cognitive computing technology, not a specific machine. The same A.I. system is used in a variety of ways by many different companies.

This doctor is using a tablet computer to access the *Watson Health* database.

Getting rich through A.I.

People with money to invest can hire *traders* to buy and sell shares in big companies. They used to use human traders, who could carry out hundreds of trades in a day. Today, computers follow trading algorithms that allow them to complete *millions* of trades every *second*.

30 years ago, Stock Exchanges were filled with frantic human traders. Today, they are home to machines called *servers* that connect computers to each other. Human traders are barely needed.

A.I. fortune tellers

Traders hire *business analysts* to make forecasts about a company's future profits or losses, based on information such as past successes and upcoming news stories. Algorithms are taking over much of this work, predicting which shares will go up or down in value, hours, days, even months ahead of time.

Intelligent machines at work	
Job description	**Mechanical upgrade already at work**
Farming, especially sowing seeds and harvesting crops	Driverless tractors pulling different equipment
Designing and manufacturing clothes	Programmable looms and sewing machines
Exploring the world – and beyond	Remote controlled probes, drones and rovers
Setting and marking homework	Online education and testing software
Security	Driverless vehicles can patrol borders and war-torn areas on land, sea and from the air
Telecommunications	Automatic exchanges connect phone calls

As machines improve and evolve, they naturally take over jobs done by human workers. Companies still need people to install, program and repair the machines – at least for now.

Getting to know you

A.I. technology can find out all sorts of things about individuals by comparing data from sensors with information on databases. The same A.I. systems that help police agencies to track crime suspects can also help stores boost their sales.

Data detectives

Today's security forces have to examine an ever-growing pool of digital data from phones, emails, street cameras and other sources. They use algorithms to hunt for patterns and key words, for example to help identify and track terrorists.

GCHQ is one of the UK's largest spy organizations. Satellites intercept phone and email data constantly. A.I. quickly sifts and sorts it all for human operators.

Personality profiling

The ultimate sales assistant would be able to tell what a customer is likely to buy as soon as he or she walks into a store, and be on hand to make a sale. Here's how sales teams might one day make use of existing A.I. technology to help...

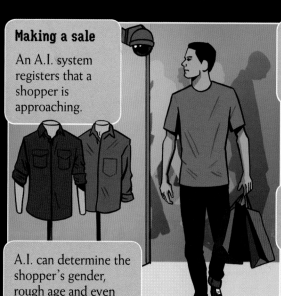

Making a sale

An A.I. system registers that a shopper is approaching.

A.I. can determine the shopper's gender, rough age and even fashion sense.

Through the shopper's phone, A.I. systems can tell if he has bought anything at the store before.

```
Age:            24
Previous
purchases:  red shoes
            sunglasses
            polo shirt
```

It can also track his movements, to see where he stops to browse.

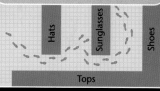

Combining all this information, A.I. could do two things:

1. Display targeted advertising designed to appeal to the shopper.

2. Share details with human sales assistants about what the shopper is likely to be interested in.

Finding faces

Most people identify and recognize each other simply by looking at their faces. Computers are still learning how to do this – but they are learning very quickly.

A face in the crowd

Police detectives are trying to find a crime suspect. They're using a facial recognition A.I. to study footage from a camera in a busy train station.

A camera captures thousands of facial images at a time.

A.I. overlays a grid onto one face...

...then adjusts the angle so the face is front on.

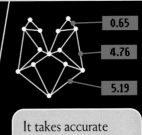

It takes accurate measurements of certain key features.

A.I. can compare each face from the camera to a photo of the suspect...

...until it finds a match.

Local police officers pursue the suspect.

Seeing through disguises

A.I. linked to video cameras and databases can even identify people when their faces are masked or out of sight. An algorithm records and analyzes the person's *gait* – their body movements as they walk or run.

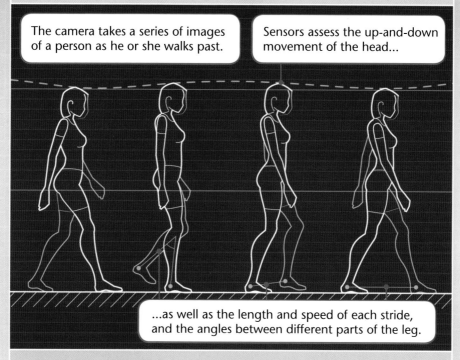

The camera takes a series of images of a person as he or she walks past.

Sensors assess the up-and-down movement of the head...

...as well as the length and speed of each stride, and the angles between different parts of the leg.

People can be identified by their gait. Some experts think they could be as unique as our fingerprints.

Relying on humans

Both methods of identification require the A.I. to link to a database that matches an image with a person's name. With access to social media websites, A.I. can build an identity database very quickly – as long as a photo has been uploaded and correctly named in the first place.

A.I. enhancements

The world's armed forces are putting A.I. into new wearable tools that protect and assist their soldiers.

Taking the weight

Machine body suits, known as *robot exoskeletons*, help a soldier carry heavy equipment over long distances. A.I. in the control unit tracks the soldier's limbs and keeps the suit moving at a safe speed and position.

This soldier is wearing a *HULC* suit. It helps to spread the weight of his gear as he walks, preventing long-term bone damage, and reduces the stress on his body when firing the gun.

Instant information

The *Q-Warrior®* headset gives a soldier a transparent display lens over one eye. A.I. links the soldier to other cameras, sensors and troops around the battlefield, showing them night vision images, their location in the world and a constantly updating map of all friendly and hostile forces.

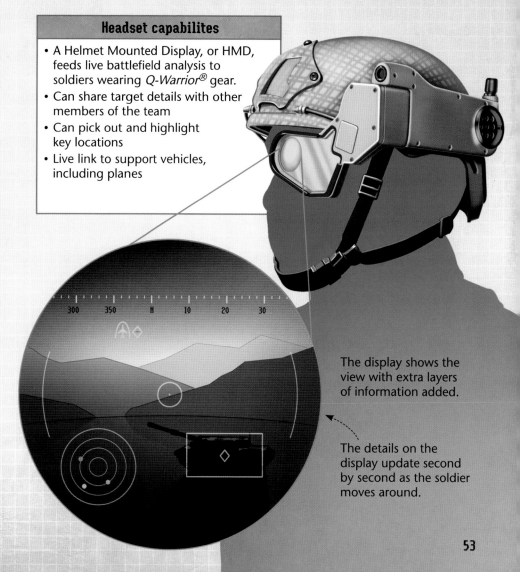

Headset capabilites

- A Helmet Mounted Display, or HMD, feeds live battlefield analysis to soldiers wearing *Q-Warrior®* gear.
- Can share target details with other members of the team
- Can pick out and highlight key locations
- Live link to support vehicles, including planes

The display shows the view with extra layers of information added.

The details on the display update second by second as the soldier moves around.

Robot rescue

Search and rescue robots will one day be able to enter disaster sites too dangerous for human emergency service teams. They'll use A.I. to navigate the site and to interact with obstacles and survivors.

Fit for humans

Humanoid robots are deliberately designed with limbs so that their A.I. can assess the site from the point of view of any human survivors needing to escape.

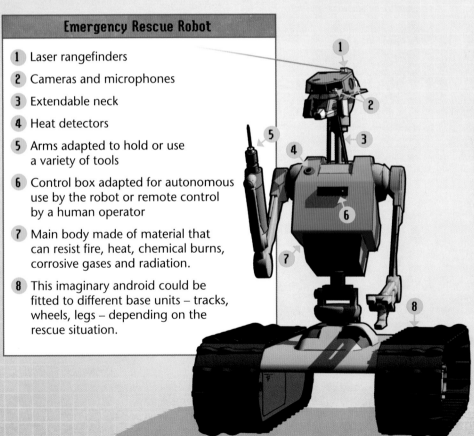

Emergency Rescue Robot

1. Laser rangefinders
2. Cameras and microphones
3. Extendable neck
4. Heat detectors
5. Arms adapted to hold or use a variety of tools
6. Control box adapted for autonomous use by the robot or remote control by a human operator
7. Main body made of material that can resist fire, heat, chemical burns, corrosive gases and radiation.
8. This imaginary android could be fitted to different base units – tracks, wheels, legs – depending on the rescue situation.

First responder

This robot is running a test. It has to navigate its way through a bombed-out building and rescue any human survivors.

HELP!

Its humanoid body can climb over debris...

...duck and crawl under obstacles...

...open doors...

...and carry heavy objects, including people.

This rescue robot is even able to drive a car, to get the person to safety as fast as possible.

A safer ride

Self-driving test cars fitted with sensors and A.I. have already completed thousands of accident-free journeys on our roads. They promise safer, faster and cleaner transportation for all of us.

Mercedes–Benz *F 015 Luxury in Motion*
(Germany, in development)

- **Intended use:** an autonomous car that functions as a living space, as well as form of transportation

What the car knows

The car knows its location in the world, and its exact position on the road.

It can decide when to stop and start, and plan its own routes.

It can see and understand traffic lights and other signals.

It can monitor moving objects around it, such as other cars, and even predict how they will move.

Real-time traffic updates

The main computer in a driverless car checks and combines information from all its sensors hundreds of times a second. A form of weak A.I. allows the computer to predict road conditions and adjust its driving to match.

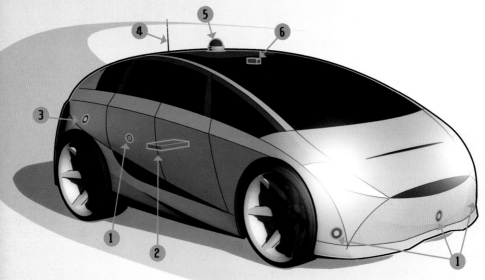

1 RADAR
Radio waves can track the speed of nearby moving things, from other cars to bicycles and pedestrians.

2 CPU
A Central Processing Unit – part of the main computer – combines and interprets information from each sensor, and controls the car.

3 Ultrasonic sensors
Sensors at ground level help the car navigate narrow places, such as parking spaces.

4 GPS tracker
A Global Positioning System allows the CPU to monitor where the car is, and plot routes, by connecting to GPS satellites.

5 LIDAR
Rotating, roof-mounted sensors use lasers to determine the distance of objects up to 200m (650ft) away.

6 Camera
(including Infra Red camera) Video cameras can track and understand road signs, such as speed restrictions.

Benefits	Risks
• A.I. will never get tired or distracted • Programmed to drive for maximum fuel efficiency • Will never get lost • Allows all passengers in a car to do other things on a journey	• Not clear who is responsible for the car – the owner, the manufacturer, or the A.I. software creator • Insurance laws will need to change • Risk of electronic failure could be catastrophic

Pods on trial

Some of the first driverless cars to be tested in a busy city are these pods, based on a design used to carry passengers around Heathrow Airport in London, UK.

Getting off the ground

Aircraft design has always made use of the latest technology. A.I. systems in a passenger jet collect sensor information and help pilots to fly safely even through extreme weather.

Hands-off flying

The *autoflight* A.I. in a passenger jet can control and even land a plane. But human pilots can land more smoothly, and only use it in thick fog, when the A.I.'s sensors give it an advantage over human eyesight.

The autoflight controls keep this Boeing 607 on course while the pilot is talking to air traffic control.

Flying acrobats

Machines that can move around without needing a human controller are known as *autonomous vehicles*. Engineers have combined autonomous drones with A.I. systems that can keep track of their own position in the air.

So far, self-tracking, autonomous drones only work within a testing lab.

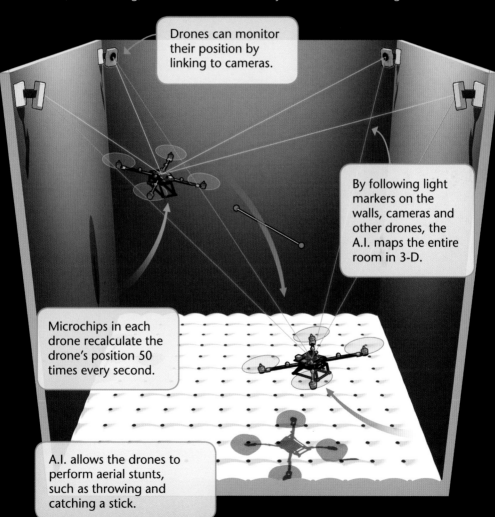

Drones can monitor their position by linking to cameras.

By following light markers on the walls, cameras and other drones, the A.I. maps the entire room in 3-D.

Microchips in each drone recalculate the drone's position 50 times every second.

A.I. allows the drones to perform aerial stunts, such as throwing and catching a stick.

A.I. in space

Space exploration is our greatest engineering challenge and A.I. is already a vital tool in the mission to learn about other worlds.

This is the Mars rover *Curiosity*. A.I. gives it the independence to select its own route across the Red Planet's rocky surface and to identify objects for closer study.

Space android

Unlike astronauts, robots don't need to sleep, exercise or wear bulky spacesuits. Onboard the International Space Station, *Robonaut 2* can copy the movements of a human controller, even turning dials and using complex machinery.

Robonaut 2, mounted on a pedestal, is learning how to communicate with operatives on Earth using sign language.

Astronauts can control Robonaut 2 directly, or set a task and let the robot's A.I. find the best solution.

Learning from stories

Science fiction authors, many of them working scientists, have written stories imagining how the world might change if machines ever became as smart – or smarter – than humans. These ideas have helped engineers to explore new pathways towards A.I., even though many of the stories warn of terrible dangers.

Frankenstein
Mary Shelley (1818)

Doctor Victor Frankenstein creates an artificial living being using body parts shocked to life by electricity.

Although the creature is intelligent and wants to make friends, Victor is horrified by it. He turns it away, setting off a cycle of violence and revenge.

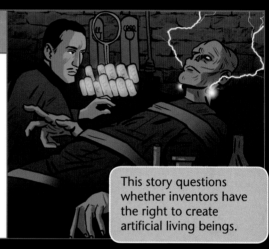

This story questions whether inventors have the right to create artificial living beings.

The Pedestrian
Ray Bradbury (1951)

A man is out for a late night stroll, when he is stopped by a driverless A.I. police car.

The A.I. can't understand that someone might want to go for a walk with no particular purpose, and so arrests the pedestrian.

This story revolves around the difficulty of translating human ways of thinking into a set of logical algorithms.

A 1927 movie called *Metropolis* is, partly, an adaptation of the story of Frankenstein. Mad doctor Rotwang creates an android using brainwaves from a woman named Maria. Rotwang hopes his creation will bring order to society but instead, like Frankenstein's monster, the android wreaks havoc.

A leap of imagination

In the 1950s, American computer scientist John McCarthy gathered a panel of engineers and designers to discuss the future of thinking machines. Their meeting at Dartmouth College, New Hampshire, is a milestone in the story of A.I.

Cognitive scientist Marvin Minsky was one of the first of the group to build a creative machine – a robot hand that could construct a tower using blocks.

Camera

Arm with claw

Minsky believed that his robot proved machines do not need human-level intelligence to do a creative job.

Meanwhile, in the UK in 1948, brain scientist William Grey Walter designed one of the first ever machines with simple A.I., two roughly tortoise-shaped robots named *Elmer* and *Elsie*.

Motors and wheels allowed the tortoise to move around on its own.

Light sensor

Both robots could move by themselves. They were designed to follow a light source.

Grey Walter found this simple command – follow the light – was enough to let the robots navigate around obstacles, and even to dance around each other.

Blowing hot and cold

In the 1950s and 60s, new breakthroughs in A.I. research came every month. But progress stalled in the 1970s, when companies and governments stopped investing in research. This led to a period known as the *A.I. Winter*.

New breakthroughs such as A.I. successes in *chess* and *go* have renewed public interest, but most experts believe we are a long way from creating a true 'thinking machine'.

Fresh thinking

One way that an A.I. can take on a simple-sounding task, such as recognizing a person's expression, is to follow a set of stored instructions, and compare it to data gained as it tries the task. The A.I. plots its own algorithms called *decision trees*.

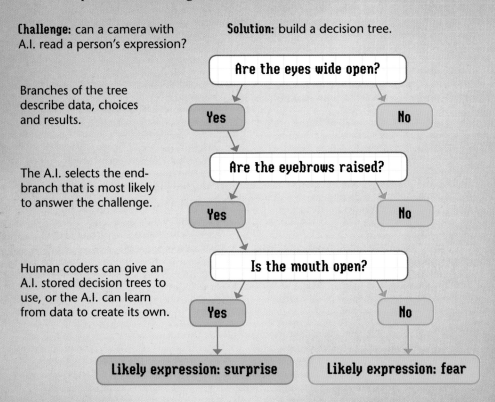

Challenge: can a camera with A.I. read a person's expression?

Solution: build a decision tree.

Branches of the tree describe data, choices and results.

Are the eyes wide open?
Yes
No

The A.I. selects the end-branch that is most likely to answer the challenge.

Are the eyebrows raised?
Yes
No

Human coders can give an A.I. stored decision trees to use, or the A.I. can learn from data to create its own.

Is the mouth open?
Yes
No

Likely expression: surprise
Likely expression: fear

A wider net

Some problems have too many possible outcomes or don't suit the rules of decision trees. For these, coders turn to another form of A.I. called artificial neural networks, or *ANNs*, that imitate the web of neurons in the human brain.

ANNs are made up of thousands or millions of individual A.I. inputs, all working together to understand which responses lead to the best results. An ANN learns by itself, not by following a coder's program. Engineers use ANNs for the most difficult – and ambitious – A.I. challenges.

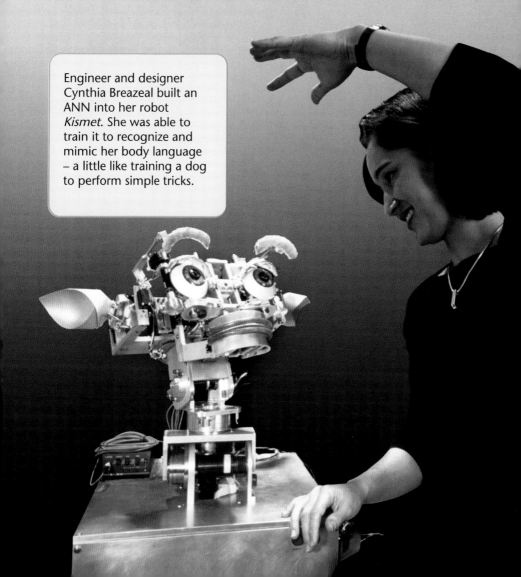

Engineer and designer Cynthia Breazeal built an ANN into her robot *Kismet*. She was able to train it to recognize and mimic her body language – a little like training a dog to perform simple tricks.

The long reach of A.I.

A.I. has the potential to change and improve every aspect of our lives, offering new ways to travel, exciting breakthroughs in technology, and even improved entertainment and healthcare.

What A.I. may do for us in the future	
Better travel	Create a fully automated driverless transportation network, minimizing accidents, delays, or getting lost.
Better entertainment	Generate satisfying music and stories without getting writer's block – and to provide tailor-made virtual reality environments to enjoy them in.
Better government	Run entire countries, for example controlling the economy and security forces. In theory, they would be programmed to be equally fair to all people.
Better standards of living	Carry out all the work that nobody wants to do, as well as doing it faster and better.
Better health	Install tiny robots, called *nanobots*, fitted with A.I., inside our bodies.

Healthcare nanobots may be able to identify and repair damage inside and out almost instantaneously. This should allow people to live incredibly long and healthy lives, perhaps cheating death itself.

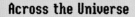

Across the Universe

Science fiction has already predicted an A.I. invention known as the *von Neumann probe*, a machine that could scour the most distant galaxies searching for a new home for humanity.

An A.I. housed inside a robotic space probe travels to an alien planet...

...where it mines the resources needed to build, and fuel, a fleet of new probes.

Each new probe finds it own new planet, where it can build new probes...

Some probes are likely to find planets fit for humans, and could even help design spacecraft to carry people across vast distances to reach them.

Beyond human concerns

A.I. is intended to be a tool to help people. But experts fear that unless machines understand what it *means* to help people – a concept that may be impossible to write into an algorithm – strong A.I. might result in a new worldwide extinction event: our own.

Robot revolution

With the rapid advances in A.I., many experts are convinced that machine intelligence will, one day, far outstrip human intelligence. Superintelligent robots may decide that they should be in charge of people – not the other way around.

Superintelligent robots will operate at speeds far, far faster than human brains. Some experts suggest such machines would think of humans the way we think of snails.

There are already more smart phones than people on planet Earth. One day, androids built as companions or servants may come to outnumber humans, too.

Robot rights

A machine with human-level intelligence could be described as being alive.

If a person switched such a machine off, would that count as murder? If people put these machines to work without paying them, would that be slavery?

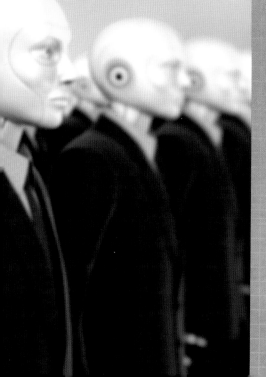

Isaac Asimov
(1920–1992)

American biochemist and author Isaac Asimov wrote many stories about robots.

In the 1940s he set down his laws of *robotics* (a word he created) that would ensure robots couldn't harm humans. But his stories often showed how his own laws might fail.

Asimov's Laws of Robotics

1. A robot may not harm a human or, through inaction, allow a human to be harmed.

2. A robot must obey orders given by humans except where they conflict with the First Law.

3. A robot must protect itself as long as such protection does not conflict with the First or Second Law.

This robot, known as *Roboy Junior*, is a prototype designed to improve understanding of how robots can better mimic humans.

Roboy Junior is working with a project to help a digital brain experience the world through a physical body.

A brave new world

The pursuit of A.I. has already led to breathtaking achievements. Many experts believe we are just decades away from a new age of A.I., when machines will attain a level of intelligence that could equal and assist our own.

If we can build safeguards into superintelligent machines, they might open up a new chapter for the human race.

A.I. on the internet

For links to websites where you can see robots interacting with people, try simple coding challenges that make robots move and watch clips from RoboCup, go to the Usborne Quicklinks website at **www.usborne.com/quicklinks** and enter the keywords: **artificial intelligence**.

Glossary

This glossary explains some of the words used in this book. If a word is written in *italic* type, it has an entry of its own.

algorithm A series of instructions that tell a *computer* or *robot* what to do.

android A *humanoid robot* that is almost indistinguishable from a human being.

autonomous Machines that can move around by themselves, without needing a human operator.

coder Someone who writes programs or *algorithms*.

computer A machine that can be programmed to follow a variety of different sets of instructions.

data Information, especially as stored on a *computer*.

drone An unmanned flying machine, piloted by a remote control, or *autonomously* using its own onboard sensors and guidance system.

hardware The physical parts of a *robot* or *computer*.

humanoid robot A robot with the basic shape and face of a human being.

neural network A large collection of *neurons, sensors* or *algorithms* working together to process *data*.

neuron A brain cell that shares and interprets information.

probe A machine designed to explore different environments, and report back with its findings.

robot Any machine that carries out a complex series of tasks by itself.

rover A *robot* that can move along the ground, often on wheels or tracks.

sensor A device that records information about the physical world.

smartphone A phone that can connect to the internet, often able to perform tasks that require *weak A.I.*

software The coded information that helps *robots* and *computers* to carry out different tasks.

strong A.I. Also known as general A.I., *software* that would allow a machine to learn how to perform mutiple tasks; potentially indistinguishable from human intelligence.

supercomputer Computers capable of incredible speed and data storage.

superintelligence A.I. that far exceeds human intelligence – generally believed not to exist yet.

weak A.I. Also known as narrow A.I., *software* that gives machines the ability to solve basic problems.

A.I. in fiction

Experts argue about whether or not it will ever be possible to create a truly intelligent machine, that could pass for human. But people have been fascinated by the idea for decades. The stories in this list all explore the implications of A.I. in today's world, and in a possible future.

Darwin among the Machines
(Samuel Butler, 1868) Short story describing a world in which machines have evolved without human input.

I, Robot (Isaac Asimov, 1950) Collection of short stories exploring Asimov's Three Laws of Robotics.

Colossus (D.F. Jones, 1966) A computer scientist connects an A.I. to the U.S. government's weapons system, hoping to achieve world peace.

2001: A Space Odyssey
(Arthur C. Clarke and Stanley Kubrik, 1968) A computer with A.I. argues with an astronaut during a space mission.

Do Androids Dream of Electric Sheep?
(Philip K. Dick, 1968) A detective struggles to determine the difference between androids and human beings.

The Hitch-Hiker's Guide to the Galaxy
(Douglas Adams, 1978) A superintelligent A.I. finds the answer to the meaning of life, but needs to create an even cleverer A.I. to explain it to humans.

When HARLIE was 1 (David Gerrold, 1978) A psychologist helps an A.I. learn what it is to be human.

RoboHunter: Verdus
(John Wagner and Ian Gibson, 1978) Comic series in which a human detective tries to persuade a planet of robots that he is, in fact, a human being.

D.A.R.Y.L. (Simon Wincer, 1985) An android in the shape of a young boy hides out from the government agency that created him.

Hyperion (Dan Simmons, 1989) In a future society, humans must decide whether to trust a group of superintelligent A.I.s known as the TechnoCore.

Sim City / The Sims (Will Wright, 1989) Game in which players set up virtual cities and families that interact together in realistic ways.

A.I. Artificial Intelligence
(Steven Spielberg, 2001) An android boy learns what it is to be a robot, but longs to become a human.

Wall·E (Andrew Stanton, 2008) The last robot on Earth helps rescue humanity from ecological disaster.

Ex Machina (Alex Garland, 2015) An inventor invites a coder to find out if his new android can pass an advanced version of the Turing Test.

Index

Acknowledgements

Every effort has been made to trace and acknowledge ownership of copyright. If any rights have been omitted, the publishers offer to rectify this in any future editions following notification. The publishers are grateful to the following individuals and organizations for permission to feature and reproduce material on the following pages:

cover © Science Picture Co / Science Photo Library; **p1** © Science Photo Library / Getty Images; **p2-3** © Reuters / Yuya Shino ; **p4** © Oliver Burston / Alamy Stock Photo; **p5** © Alfred Pasieka / Science Photo Library; **p7** © Detlev van Ravenswaay / Science Photo Library; **p8-9** © Bloomberg / Getty Images; **p11** © Long Hongtao / Xinhua Press / Corbis; **p16** © Musee d'Art et d'Histoire, Neuchatel, Switzerland / Bridgeman Images; **p17** © World History Archive / Alamy Stock Photo; **p18** © Mary Evans Picture Library; **p19 (top)** © Alberto Estevez / epa / Corbis, with thanks to Honda North America; **(bottom)** © AFP / Yoshikazu Tsuno / Getty Images, *Pepper* created by Aldebaran; **p20** © Science Museum / Science & Society Picture Library; **p22 (Turing)** © famouspeople / Alamy Stock Photo, **(von Neumann)** © George Karger / Getty Images; **p23** Crown Copyright by kind permission GCHQ; **p26 (valve)** © Zoonar GmbH / Alamy Stock Photo, **(transistor)** © Ivan Sizov / Alamy Stock Photo, **(Kilby circuit)** © Andrew Burton / Getty Images; **p27** © Science & Society Picture Library / Getty Images; **p28-29** © Picture Alliance/Photoshot; **p30** © AFP Photo / ANP / Bart Maat; **p31** © 2016 Atari Interactive, Inc.; **p32 (headset)** © Sony Computer Entertainment Inc; **p32-33** © PlayStation; **p34-35** © Jens Schlueter / Getty Images, *NAO* created by Aldebaran; **p36 (Zoomer puppy)** TM & © Spin Master Ltd. All Rights Reserved, **(Dino)** With thanks to CogniToy, **(Tamagotchi)** With thanks to Bandai; **p37** © Shizuo Kambayashi/AP/Press Association Images; **p38 (top)** *Pepper* created by Aldebaran, **(bottom)** with thanks to Hanson Robotics; **p39** © Reuters / Tyrone Siu, with thanks to Hanson Robotics; **p42-43** © Arnd Wiegmann / Reuters / Corbis; **p43** © AFP Photo / Yoshikazu Tsuno; **p44** © 2016 Intuitive Surgical, Inc. Used with permission; **p45 (top)** with thanks to Toyohashi University of Technology, **(middle)** with thanks to Sumitomo Riko Company Limited, **(bottom)** Courtesy of International Business Machines Corporation, © (2015) International Business Machines Corporation. IBM Watson is a trademark of IBM Corp, registered in many jurisdictions worldwide; **p46 (Main)** © Christoph Schmidt / EPA / Corbis, **(inset)** © Charles Bennett / AP / Press Association Images; **p48** © Adrian Sherratt / Alamy Stock Photo; **p52** © 2016 Photo Courtesy of Lockheed Martin; **p53** *Q-Warrior*® is a registered trade mark of BAE Systems plc and is used here with permission; **p56-57** © David Becker / Getty Images; **p59** © Tim Jones / Alamy Stock Photo; **p60** © Kent Wien / Getty Images; **p62-63 (Robonaut 2)** © NASA; **p65** © Photos 12 / Alamy Stock Photo; **p66** Courtesy MIT Museum; **p67** © Robots and automatons, Division of Work & Industry, National Museum of American History, Smithsonian Institution; **p69** © Sam Ogden / Science Photo Library; **p72-73** © iLexx / Getty Images; **p73** © Mondadori Portfolio / Getty Images; **p74-75** © Roboy Project, A.I. Lab, University of Zurich, 27.2.2013, Photography: Adrian Baer

With thanks to Edward Grefenstette for expert advice
Additional illustrations by Jamie 313 @ KJA artists
Series editor: Jane Chisholm   Series designers: Zoe Wray and Neil Francis
Digital design by John Russell   Picture research by Ruth King